SOCCER

David **M**arshal

RIGBY
INTERACTIVE
LIBRARY

Printed in the United States of America

00 99 98 97 96
10 9 8 7 6 5 4 3 2 1

Library of Congress Cataloging-in-Publication Data
Marshall, David, 1945 Mar. 12–
    Soccer / David Marshall.
        p. cm. -- (Successful sports)
    Includes index.
    ISBN 1-57572-069-8 (library)
    1. Socer--Juvenile literature. 2. Soccer--Rules--Juvenile literature.
    3. Soccer players--Juvenile literature. I. Title. II. Series.
GV943.25.M27 1996

796.334 ' 2--dc20
96-13819
CIP
AC

Acknowledgments
The publishers would like to thank the following for permission
to reproduce photographs:
Action-plus: p. 11; Allsport: pp. 4, 18, 23, 27, 31; Allsport/© Shaun
Boterrill: front cover, pp. 8, 20; Allsport/Chris Cole: p. 13; Allsport/
Stephen Dunn: p. 28; AP Wirephoto: p. 11; Colorsport: pp. 7, 9, 18,
20; Empics: p. 26; David Madison: pp. 12, 27; John Morrison: p. 17;
Ivor Nicholas: p. 28; PhotoEdit/© Amy C. Etra: p. 23; PhotoEdit/
David Young-Wolff: p. 14; Meg Sullivan and
Andrew Waters: pp. 17, 21.

Illustrator:
Stephen Brayfield: p. 6, 9, 15, 17, 25

Visit Rigby's
Education Station®
on the
World Wide Web at
http://www.rigby.com

Contents

The Basics of Soccer

Goal!—no matter where you are in the world, everyone knows what this word means. The game of soccer, or **Association Football**, is known as "the people's game," and is the world's most popular team sport. Nearly every country plays soccer in some form.

Soccer's popularity stems from its simple purpose—to put a ball into the other team's goal, using only the feet, head or body, and to stop opponents from doing the same to you. Most of the rules are easy to understand, and any number can play. However, organized games are between two teams of eleven players.

The rules issued by the game's governing body, **FIFA** (*Fédération Internationale de Football Association*), say that soccer should be played on a rectangular field between 100 to 130 yards long and 50 to 100 yards wide. A goal is placed at each end of the field and has to be 8 yards wide and 8 feet high. Lines at the sides of the field mark the touchlines; those at each end are the goal lines. The halfway line, the goal areas, the penalty areas, the corners, the center circle and the penalty spots are also marked. Corners are marked with flags.

No matter what shape you are—short and stocky, or tall and thin—you can enjoy playing soccer.

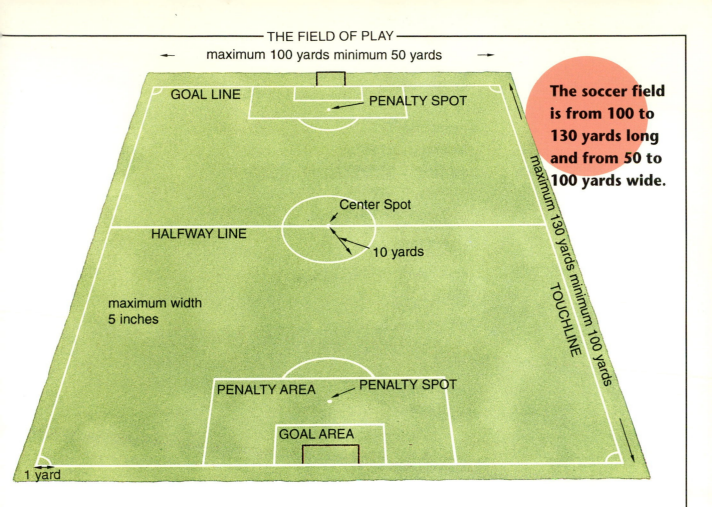

maximum 100 yards minimum 50 yards

GOAL LINE

PENALTY SPOT

The soccer field is from 100 to 130 yards long and from 50 to 100 yards wide.

Center Spot

HALFWAY LINE

10 yards

maximum 130 yards minimum 100 yards

TOUCHLINE

maximum width 5 inches

PENALTY AREA

PENALTY SPOT

GOAL AREA

1 yard

The ball must be 27 to 28 inches around and should weigh from 14 to 16 ounces at the beginning of the game. Modern white soccer balls are made of waterproof leather and will weigh the same at the end of a game as at the beginning. In the past, brown leather balls would soak up water and double in weight on wet, muddy days.

The player's uniform consists of a shirt, shorts, socks, shoes, and usually shin guards. To prevent the players from falling when they twist and turn, the shoes have cleats on the soles. These cleats must be changed before they break and become a danger to other players. It is one task of the three officials who are also on the field—the **referee** and two **linespersons**—to make sure that no player has equipment that will injure another player.

Pointers

Tie your shoelaces so the knot is on top of your foot, so when you pass the ball the knot won't slip to one side and change the ball's direction.

Playing the Game

The game is divided into two halves, each lasting 45 minutes. The break at half-time should last about 10 minutes. There should be 90 minutes of actual play. The clock generally does not stop in a soccer game unless a player is injured or other special circumstances occur, such as making **substitutions.** At the end of the game, the officials decide how much extra time should be played to allow for game delays that have occurred while the clock was still running.

Before the game starts, the captain of the home team tosses a coin and allows the other captain to call. Whoever wins the toss can decide whether to **kick off** and choose which end to defend in the first half.

Pointers

After the kick-off, concentrate and keep your eye on the ball. When you receive it decide what you are going to do — and be positive.

The players, ready for kick-off.

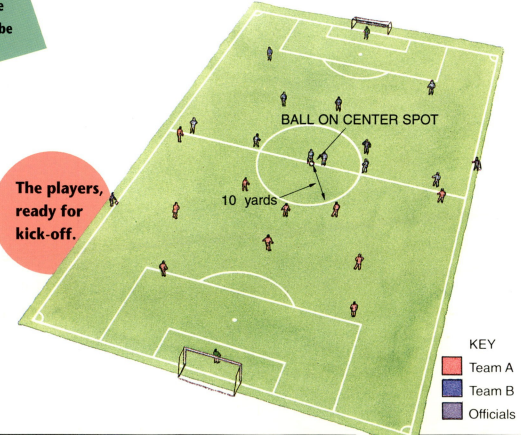

BALL ON CENTER SPOT

10 yards

KEY

Team A

Team B

Officials

As play begins, the team in possession of the ball tries to advance to the opposing team's goal, while the other team does its best to prevent them. In soccer, touching the ball with the hands is not permitted, so players use a variety of techniques to move the ball, steal the ball, and score goals. Most ball handling is done with the feet, though players also use their head, knees, and chest.

Ruud Gullit of Holland and Lothar Matthäus of West Germany, the two opposing captains, shake hands and exchange emblems before the start of a game in the 1990 World Cup.

Kicking is the most important skill in soccer. Players use various kicking techniques to pass the ball to a teammate and to score goals. They usually kick the ball so that it travels just above the grass. However, sometimes when passing the ball, a player may choose to kick it over the head of an opposing player. While the ball is high in the air, heading it, or striking it with the head, may be the only way to get control of it. Players use **heading** to pass the ball, intercept it, or shoot at the goal.

Dribbling, in which a player nudges the ball along the ground with the feet, is another important skill. By dribbling, a player can keep possession of the ball while running. To steal a ball from the opposing team, a player may use the feet to kick or snatch it away while standing, or may slide along the ground with one leg extended and kick the ball away. These moves are called **tackling**.

The Defense

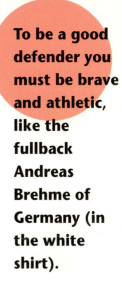

To succeed at the top level, soccer players have to acquire many skills. They need to be able to control the ball and balance and turn while running fast. And they should be fit, quick-thinking in order to anticipate what will happen next, and not be afraid to get involved.

There are usually four defenders, often called *fullbacks,* stationed near their team's goal, whose job it is to stop the other side from scoring. Players on defense must have the strength to tackle firmly, and speed to match the opposing attackers. Central defenders must be able to head the ball well. Sometimes a team will have an extra defender who stays at the back behind the rest of the defense. This player is known as a "sweeper" because his or her aim is to sweep up any attackers left uncovered or any loose balls that get through the defense. The sweeper can also break through the middle to join the attack.

To be a good defender you must be brave and athletic, like the fullback Andreas Brehme of Germany (in the white shirt).

There are many different ways for players to defend. The most obvious way is known as man-to-man coverage. When attackers get near the goal, it is important that each member of the attacking team is covered by someone on defense. If a player is left uncovered then it will be easy to score. Man-to-man coverage is always used when defending corner kicks or free kicks. Sometimes, teams use man-to-man coverage for a whole game.

A different method of defending is the zone defense. This means that each player defends a certain area of the field, or zone, when defenders cannot follow when an attacker leaves their zone.

An important point to remember is that it is better to give up a throw-in or a corner kick than a goal. If a player is trapped with the ball close to his or her own goal, it is better to kick it out of play than try to dribble it out of trouble. As a defender, you should also try to get yourself between the attacker and your goal. If the attacker is on your goal side, then he or she is already in a position to score.

A good way of practicing defending is to get a friend to run around with the ball at his or her feet, changing speed and direction as often as possible. Meanwhile you try to run alongside, keeping as close as you can. You can also put the ball on the ground and run as fast as you can toward it, sliding into a tackle as you reach it.

The main reason Des Walker of England was voted the best defender at the World Cup in 1990 was his terrific speed.

The Midfield

Young players often ask if they can play in midfield. This is because midfield players are the complete all-purpose players of the game. They have to be able to move toward their own goal and help the defense, and move forward to try to score goals. They are also known as the "creators"—the players who have to be able to pass the ball accurately over short and long distances. The midfield is often known as the "engine room" of the game because it is where all the hard work takes place. Midfield players are always involved.

When watching a game, you will often see the midfield players looking up to see who they can pass to. They have to know what is going on around them. TV commentators say that some players have a 'vision' of what is happening on the field. This vision is what enables some of the best midfielders to be in the right place at the right time.

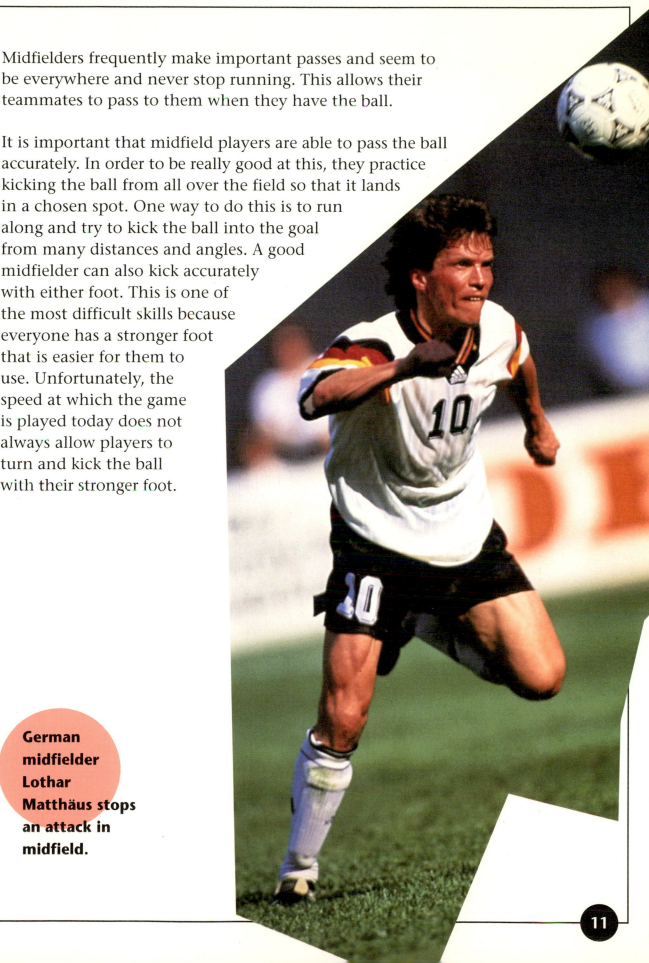

Midfielders frequently make important passes and seem to be everywhere and never stop running. This allows their teammates to pass to them when they have the ball.

It is important that midfield players are able to pass the ball accurately. In order to be really good at this, they practice kicking the ball from all over the field so that it lands in a chosen spot. One way to do this is to run along and try to kick the ball into the goal from many distances and angles. A good midfielder can also kick accurately with either foot. This is one of the most difficult skills because everyone has a stronger foot that is easier for them to use. Unfortunately, the speed at which the game is played today does not always allow players to turn and kick the ball with their stronger foot.

German midfielder Lothar Matthäus stops an attack in midfield.

The Strikers

Easily the greatest thrill when playing a game of soccer is scoring a goal. Watching a goal being scored is almost as good! Most teams have two or three players whose main job is to try to score. From their different positions on the field players dribble the ball by controlling it with their feet, and pass it to one another as they advance toward their opponents' goal. They often play for most of the game on one side of the field or the other. They are known as "wingers." Other players stay mainly in the center—these are called "strikers" because their job is to score goals.

In order to be a good striker, you have to be able to score goals no matter how the ball comes to you. In almost every game you will see a striker dive to head the ball, or kick the ball over his head, or shoot at the goal "first-time." The ability to **volley**, or kick the ball while it is in the air, is often made to look easy by the best players. In fact, it is very difficult and requires hours of practice.

Also if the ball is played to a striker in the air, he or she has to be able to head the ball well. Again, this is not an easy skill to master. To be accurate when heading the ball, a player must always meet the ball with the forehead, with the eyes open. Using your forehead reduces the danger of injury.

SOCCER FACTS

In league soccer each team can use two substitutes to replace players in the game from the start. Substitutes are used to improve the team's performance, or replace injured players. A substituted player cannot rejoin the game. A player who has been sent off cannot be substituted.

It is important to practice shooting. If there are two or three players, this is easy and fun. Practicing shooting balls into a goal can be done by putting the balls on either side of the goal about 30 feet away, and then passing them at different heights and speeds to a player running forward. This can also be good passing practice, or weaker foot practice, for those not shooting. Keeping the knee over the ball when shooting keeps the ball down and stops it from flying over the goal.

The greatest goal scorer in the history of the game was the Brazilian Pelé. In his career he scored 1,281 goals in 1,363 games. No other soccer player has scored 1,000 goals in a career.

Pelé made his debut in the World Cup competition in 1956 when he was only 16. He won his first World Cup championship in 1958, when he scored twice to help Brazil defeat Sweden. In 1975, Pelé was the first player to sign a major contract with an American professional team when he joined the New York Cosmos of the North American Soccer League.

Probably the greatest player the game has ever known — Pelé. When he scored his 1000th goal in 1969 he was already a football legend.

The Goalkeeper

The goalkeeper is probably the most important member of any team. Goalkeepers have most of the responsibility for keeping the ball out of the goal. Their position is also the most dangerous on the field. Because goalkeepers can, and must, get the ball in their hands, they often have to bend down to the feet of other players who are trying to kick it.

Goalkeepers must have quick reactions and good concentration. One minute, they might be standing getting cold with nothing to do while play is at the other end of the field, when suddenly the other team starts a threatening attack. At this point they must spring into action. If a goalkeeper runs off the goal line toward the attackers, the opposition has to shoot wider and is more likely to miss.

Goalkeepers are often the most noisy players on the field. Because they stand watching the game for minutes on end they can see things that their busier teammates have missed. They can, and often do, shout directions to other players.

A goalkeeper must get down and smother the ball when making a save.

The goal keeper is the only player who is allowed to touch the ball with the hands or arms. When stopping or catching a ball, a goalkeeper always tries to get his or her body between the ball and the goal. If a jump or dive is necessary to catch the ball, goalkeepers will pull the ball into their body as soon as possible for safety. To practice this, goalkeepers can throw or kick the ball against a wall and catch it on the rebound. Because goalkeepers must not drop the ball, they often wear gloves for a firmer grip. It is important to practice with gloves on before using them in a game to get used to them.

In the 1992–1993 season, the rules about passing back to the goalkeeper were changed. The aim was to stop defenders from wasting time by passing the ball back to their own goalkeeper, who would then pick it up to start the play again. The new rule says the goalkeeper cannot pick the ball up if a defender passes the ball back to him or her with a kick. This means the goalkeeper has to kick the ball from the ground—often with an attacker running toward it. As a result, the game has speeded up. If a player heads, rather than kicks, the ball back to their own goalkeeper then the goalkeeper can still catch it.

SOCCER FACTS

Research carried out during the 1984–1985 season showed there was a 29 per cent chance of at least one player being seriously injured in every game. That means one bad injury occurs every three or four games.

Throw-ins, Goal Kicks, and Corners

Sometimes when you are watching or playing a game of soccer, it seems that the game is being stopped for one reason or another every few seconds. Sometimes this is because of a **foul**, but often it is because the ball goes off the field, or out of play. Although this can break up the game, it can give good opportunities to attack.

The defenders often have no option but to kick the ball out of bounds. If a player kicks the ball over the touchline, then the other team takes a throw-in. Any player can take the throw. The ball must be thrown back into play two-handed from behind the player's head.

If an attacking player is the last person to touch the ball as it goes over the goal line, then a goal kick is awarded to the defending team. A goal kick is taken from within the goal area. Usually, the goalkeeper just kicks the ball as far upfield as possible. If a defender is the last player to kick the ball as it goes over the goal line, then a corner kick is awarded to the attacking team.

The ball must go back right behind the head when taking a throw-in – otherwise it is a foul throw.

When a corner kick is taken, it is important for the defenders to keep close and cover all the attacking team players.

A corner kick must be taken from the corner of the field nearest to where the ball went off. Players cannot be offside from a throw-in, goal kick, or corner kick.

The offside rule is the most difficult and complicated in the whole game. It is also the most controversial; hardly a game goes by without a few offside decisions that the spectators disagree with. Basically, a player is offside when the ball is played forward to him or her in the opponent's half and there are fewer than two opponents between him and the goal. This situation is complicated by the fact that offsides is called when the ball is kicked to the receiver, not when he or she gets it. The speed of many offensive players makes it hard for linespersons and referees to be sure when a player is offside. Every time a player is caught offside a free kick is awarded to the defending side. This slows the game down.

Offside
Player B is nearer the opponents' goal than the ball when player A kicks it to him. There is only one opponent (the goalkeeper) between him and the goal line.

Not offside
Player A has four opponents between him and the goal line when the ball is kicked. Player B is allowed to move in to meet the ball.

Not offside
The last player to touch the ball was an opponent so player B is not offside.

This diagram shows how the offside rule works.

Fouls

Apart from the offside rule, the most likely reason for stopping the game is because of a foul. This is covered by Law 12, Fouls and Misconduct. Any player who deliberately trips, pushes, or obstructs an opponent or touches the ball with the hands will be penalized, and a free kick will be given to the opponents. For more serious offenses that could cause injury or prevent a good attack, a direct free kick is given. This means that the team can aim the ball directly at the goal. For less serious offenses an indirect free kick is awarded, which means the ball must touch at least two players, including the player taking the kick, before going into the goal.

If a serious foul happens inside the **penalty area**, then a penalty kick is awarded. This is a free shot at goal from a mark about 12 yards away with only the goalkeeper to beat. Most professional teams have a player or two who are trained to take penalty shots.

The Doncaster Belles of England form a wall to block a shot at goal by Fulham in the Women's Football Association Cup Final in 1990.

If a foul is committed just outside the penalty area, a free kick is awarded from a good scoring position. The defending team lines up at least 10 yards away from the ball to try to stop the ball from going past them. This formation allows their goalkeeper to patrol a smaller area of the goal. To counteract this, several players have become experts at bending the ball around the line of players. They get the ball to swerve in an arc towards the goal. To swerve the ball takes a lot of practice.

If a player commits a foul that is very serious, perhaps risking injury to the opponent, then he or she will be cautioned, or receive a warning. The player's name will be written down in the referee's notebook and a yellow card will be shown. If the player goes on to commit a second foul of this type the player is shown a red card and thrown out of the game. Players today are shown the red card and sent off if they deliberately foul an opponent to prevent a goal from being scored. This has become known as the professional foul, although it is both unprofessional and unsportsmanlike.

Taking a penalty shot should be the easiest way of scoring a goal. A low, well-directed shot is the best way to take a penalty.

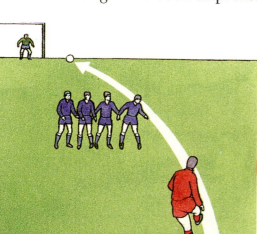

Here is how the ball travels when bent around a defensive wall.

The Referee and Linespersons

The referee's job involves blowing a whistle when play has to stop and awarding free kicks, throw-ins, and goals. The referee tries to keep the game moving and has to be as fair as possible. He or she must be able to run up and down the field with the players to see all that goes on.

Because soccer is such a fast-moving game with may players to keep track of, occasionally a referee makes a mistake. Some players take advantage of this by faking fouls. They make it look as though they have been tripped or pushed when they have not been. A referee must quickly determine whether a foul has been committed and decide on the appropriate punishment. Imagine there are just a few minutes to go in an important cup game and the score is tied. A striker falls over in the penalty area. Was he pushed? Was it a foul? Should a penalty be awarded? There might be thousands of fans yelling and screaming that a penalty should be given. The referee has just a couple of seconds to decide. If the wrong decision is made, it could change the outcome of a game.

The dreaded red card! The referee ejects a player for a professional foul.

In order for the referee and linespersons to cover the entire field, they patrol different areas. The two linespersons each watch one half of the field, each and the referee runs along an imaginary diagonal line from one corner to the other. This means there is always an official close to where the ball is being played.

The linespersons and referee carry stopwatches to keep track of the time being played. The linespersons signal to the referee when they consider each half is over. The referee then has to decide how much extra time has to be added on for stoppages. The linespersons can also indicate to the referee if they think a foul has been committed, but the referee's decision is always final. It is the linespersons' task to make sure that the referee is aware of a substitution being requested. A linesperson must also check the new player's cleats.

Sometimes, the referee will stop the game for reasons other than fouls, such as an injury or debris on the field. Afterward, the game is restarted by a drop ball. The ball is dropped between two opposing players on the spot where it was last played before the referee stopped the game. The players are not allowed to kick the ball until it has touched the ground.

After certain stoppages, the game is restarted by a drop ball.

SOCCER FACTS

Soccer has been played for many years at the college level. The National Collegiate Athletic Association (NCAA) held its first official soccer championships in 1959. The first title was won by the Pennsylvania State University Nittany Lions.

A League of Your Own

Just as every sport needs a league, soccer in the United States has the American Youth Soccer Organization (AYSO), which is the "Little League" of the sport. There are AYSO chapters, called "regions," all over the United States, in schools, park districts, and other local groups.

AYSO was founded in 1964. From the beginning, the organization has had divisions for girls as well as boys. The organization also holds clinics in its regions to provide tips on playing, learning the rules, and to help parents become good coaches and referees. But the real idea of AYSO is to make soccer a fun game. And if you want to continue playing —maybe even become a professional—AYSO can help you find the kind of competition that will improve your skills. In addition, the organization's official magazine also provides information on other regions and national competitions.

The 1994 U.S. World Cup Team. The AYSO can help young people find the kind of competition that enables some players to become pros.

The AYSO rules cover every aspect of the game, from the size of the field, to the kind of equipment that can be used, to marking the ball for a penalty kick, goal kick, corner kick, and a throw-in. Unlike hockey or basketball, in which penalties slow or even stop the game, soccer keeps moving, and slows down only slightly for penalties. But this does not mean that illegal play does not go unpunished; serious penalties that cause injury will stop the game, and the referee can eject the player who causes the injury.

The games in which young people play will likely follow AYSO rules, which are different from college or professional rules. These rules allow for substitutions, and for players to change positions during a match. These rules exist for younger players so that every member of a team can get into the game for good exercise as well as competition, and have the opportunity to play different positions.

Players at this level are probably trying to figure out which position they like best, and how they can help their team play its best. When this happens, a team plays better and the experience is fun for everybody involved. And that's what it's all about.

Claudio Gentile (6) and Dino Zoff (1) of Italy lift the World Cup after winning in 1982.

SOCCER FACTS

There are seven divisions in AYSO soccer: Under 19 (Division 1); Under 16 (Division 2); Under 14 (Division 3); Under 12 (Division 4); Under 10 (Division 5); Under 8 (Division 6); and 5 years old (Kindergarten).

Linking the Leagues

The American Youth Soccer Organization is one of the many leagues around the world that are linked together under the Federation Internationale De Football Association (FIFA), which is located in Zurich, Switzerland. Because soccer is the world's most popular sport, there are hundreds of leagues in countries on just about every continent.

Members of the various committees on rules, referees, and other parts of the game come from countries as different as Gambia, in Africa; Chile, in South America; Syria, in the Middle East, and France, Russia, and Scotland in Europe. The national headquarters of AYSO is located in Hawthorne, California.

Becoming a member of AYSO in the United States is easy, and costs only as much as your league can afford for each individual player. To learn more about it, write to AYSO, P.O. Box 5045, Hawthorne, California 90251-5045.

To become an official AYSO referee or a coach, a person must go through a lot of training and learn plenty of rules. Because of this, players can learn to respect their coaches and referees, because they really do know the game. Players can also be confident that as they move from one league into another, the type of training available and the way calls are made on the field will be consistent. It's different from baseball, in which the professional umpires call a different strike zone in the American League than they do in the National League, which is of course different from the way strikes are called in baseball games in Japan. But soccer is the same wherever it's played.

The Dutch player Ruud Gullit earned $8,250,000 after a 1987 team change.

SOCCER FACTS

Soccer is now the second-most popular sport for children in the United States. Only basketball is played by more kids, but soccer is gaining all the time. Boys make up 65 percent of the players, and girls, 35 percent.

American Alexi Lalas left a high-paying spot on a European team to help start the new U.S. pro league.

In the United States, there are 835 regions, with 525,000 young people from 4 1/2 to 18 years old playing in the leagues. But it doesn't stop there. There is also United States Amateur Football Association (USAFA) for people who continue to play soccer for the rest of their lives.

Although the main soccer seasons are in the fall and spring, there are also traveling teams that play throughout the year. So, if you have the energy and the talent, you can find a game just about anywhere, anytime.

College Kickers

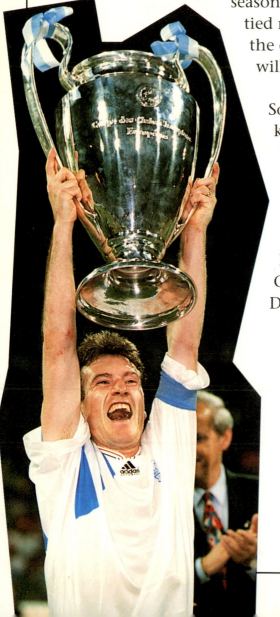

The Atlantic Coast Conference (ACC) is perhaps the most competitive in the National Collegiate Athletic Association (NCAA) Division I for basketball. What many people do not know is that it is also the most competitive college conference for soccer. College teams known for great players in sports such as basketball—Duke University and the University of Virginia, to name just two — are also among the best college soccer teams in America.

The University of Virginia Cavaliers, in fact, are the dominant team in college soccer today. They have won five NCAA titles since 1989. Their coach, Bruce Arena, started his 18th season in 1995, and has an overall 287-57-32 won-loss-tied record. On the strength of this record, he will be the coach for the 1996 U.S. Olympic soccer team that will play in Atlanta.

Soccer has become very popular at schools better known for other sports, and they are spread throughout the country. For example, the University of California at Los Angeles (UCLA), Southern Methodist University (SMU), the University of Wisconsin at Madison (UW-M) and Clemson are excellent teams. Even Ivy League schools such as Brown University and Cornell University rank in the top 12 of NCAA Division I soccer.

SOCCER FACTS

Women's college teams are just as competitive as the men's. Soccer is now the NCAA's most popular sport for women, with nearly 6,800 players on 617 teams. Women have been playing college soccer for 20 years at schools such as Notre Dame, Stanford, Duke, Texas A & M, and the University of California at San Diego. The women's soccer team at the University of North Carolina, the Tar Heels, have won 12 championships since 1982.

In many cases, women's teams are thriving where men's teams are failing because of lack of support. It is since about 1990 that women's sports now receive the kind of funding and support that have usually gone to the men's teams. As well, women are now coaching some of the best female college teams, though there are not too many women referees.

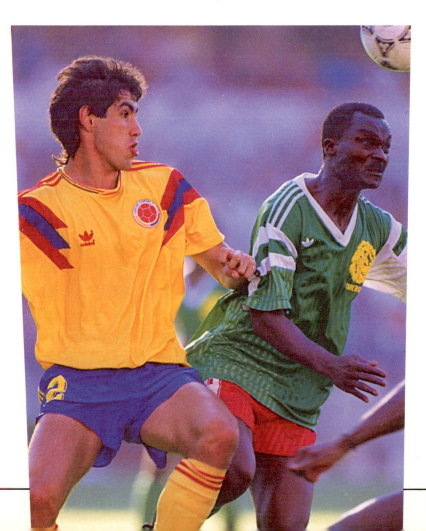

Roger Milla of Cameroon, in green, in action against Colombia in the 1990 World Cup Finals.

27

Stadiums

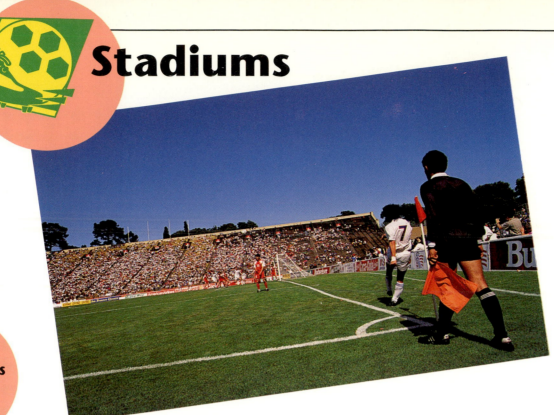

It is very exciting to stand or sit in a soccer stadium and be a part of the crowd during a game. Every mistake is booed, every success is cheered. The fans have distinctive chants and songs that are often directed at players on the field. Sometimes the crowd is like a player on the field because it can influence the way a team plays. The World Cup game in 1950 between the neighboring South American countries of Uruguay and Brazil was watched by 199,854 people in the Estadio Maracana in Rio de Janeiro. Four other games held in Rio in this tournament had crowds of more than 140,000 people. Imagine playing in those games. The shouts and cheers from such crowds must have created a powerful atmosphere.

The Estadio Maracana in Rio is still the largest soccer stadium in the world, although new grounds in the Far East are being built to rival it. The Rungnado stadium in P'yŏngyang in South Korea has a seating capacity of 150,000. The English international player Gary Lineker left his team to go and play for a Japanese team and help to develop the game there. His popularity has meant that new stadiums are being planned as the crowds begin to grow.

In the United States, there is not one major stadium devoted to soccer. It is similar to the very early days of professional football, when those teams played in stadiums that were originally designed for baseball. Even when the World Cup was played in the United States in 1994, all the teams played in stadiums that were designed for other sports.

Still, most American stadiums can be adapted for soccer, even if the fans do not always have the same opportunity to sit as closely to the action as they can in other sports. And because many American stadiums are indoors and equipped with artificial turf, it will be interesting to see how soccer in America adapts. Artificial turf is harder on legs, and creates burns from sliding.

And while it is routine for more than 60,000 people to attend a soccer game in Europe or South America—if the stadium can hold that many—that kind of attendance in the United States is usually only for playoffs or championship series, and then only for major college or professional teams.

The Pontiac Silverdome in Detroit, Michigan, is one of the most modern soccer stadiums in the world.

Soccer Highlights

People all over the world take soccer very seriously—some would say too seriously. In 1981 the ex-manager of a team in Liverpool, England, Bill Shankly, was interviewed for the London *Sunday Times* newspaper. He said: "Some people think football is a matter of life and death. I don't like that attitude. I can assure them it is much more serious than that."

Nobody knows whether he was joking or not!

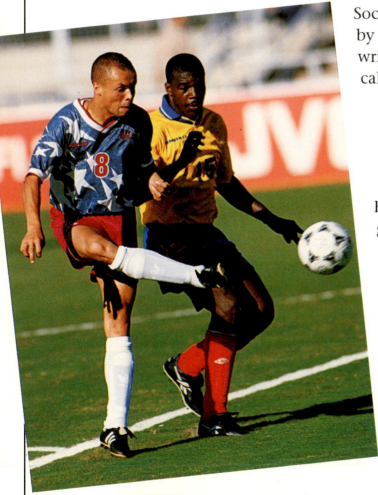

Soccer "hooliganism," or misbehavior by fans, is not a new problem. This was written by Philip Stubbes in his booklet called *Anatomie of Abuses* in 1583:

"Footeball ... causeth fighting, brawling, contention, quarrel picking, murder, homicide and great effusion of bloode, as daily experience teacheth."

He might have been describing some games of today.

The modern soccer game began in Great Britain about 150 years ago. British people spread the game all over the world—to Brazil in the 1870s, Prague and Austria in the 1880s, Russia in 1887, and Turkey in 1895. Australia played its first game in 1890, and now more than 600,000 people there play, including 20,000 women and girls. World-wide, more than 40 million people play football in more than 150 countries.

Ernie Stewart of the U.S. steals the ball from an opponent.

SOCCER FACTS

The first recorded women's organized football game was in 1895, between the northern and southern women's teams in London. In 1969 the Women's Football Association was formed. The United States won the first World Cup for Women, held in China in 1991. In June 1993, the WFA was taken over by the Football Association. There is a WFA Cup competition every year, organized by the FA. More than 12,000 women players of all ages and 450 clubs are registered with the WFA.

Soccer may be about to gain attention similar to basketball or football with the launching in 1996 of the Major Soccer League. It was scheduled to start with 10 teams in major cities such as New York, Los Angeles, Dallas, as well as Kansas City, Missouri; San Jose, California; Columbus, Ohio; Washington, D.C.; Tampa, Florida; a state-wide team in Denver, Colorado; and a regional team located in Foxboro, Massachusetts.

Most of the original players are Americans, but the league also has recruited many international players, and there will be a game of the week on a sports television network. Depending on the action of the first season, some international rules may be changed to make the game faster, or to promote higher scoring. For now, the teams will play in outdoor football stadiums.

Gill Wylie beams after securing a win in the Women's FA Cup final in 1993.

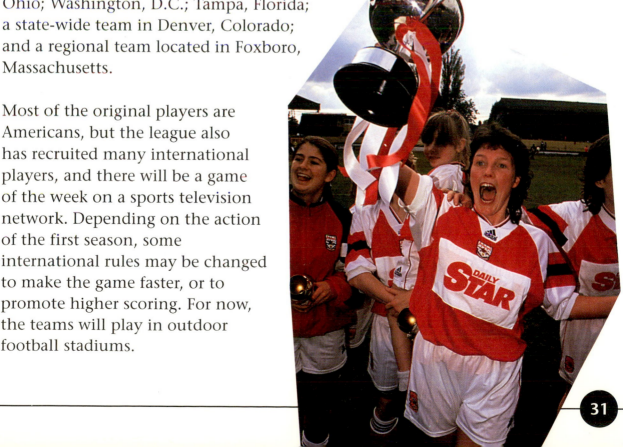

Glossary

Association Football The name of the game when first organized with rules by British teams in 1863.

corner kick When a defender is the last person to kick the ball as it goes over the goal line.

dribble A series of short kicks, usually with the side of the foot, that a player uses to move with the ball.

English Football League The first organized league in which teams played each other on a regular basis, and were awarded points for a win or draw. The first League games were played in 1888.

FIFA The Fédération Internationale de Football Association, formed in 1904, the governing body of football all over the world.

foul play Deliberately breakingr any of the game's rules.

free kick A kick given to a team for a foul against them. There are direct and indirect free kicks.

heading Hitting the ball with the head.

kick off The start of the game in which one of the teams kicks the ball forward from the center spot.

linespersons Two officials who patrol the touchlines and decide when the ball is out of play and help the referee decide on fair play.

penalties If a player is fouled within the penalty area, the team gets a penalty. These are taken directly in front of the goal, 11 m away, with only the goalkeeper in the way.

penalty area The area directly in front of the goal

promotion Teams are graded on how good they are into divisions in a league. When a team wins or is near the top in its division, it can be promoted into the next, higher division.

referee The official on the field who is in charge of the game, and who decides on start and finish times and illegal play.

substitution Bringing a player on to the field to replace someone who is injured or not playing well, or to change a team's tactics.

tackling A way of getting the ball away from an opponent, without deliberately kicking or tripping him or her.

throw in A two-handed throw from out of bounds onto the playing field that results when a player kicks the ball over the touchline.

volley When the ball is kicked in mid-air.

World Cup The international competition organized by FIFA, the final tournament of which is held every four years. Teams are put into sections from their own part of the world to play off for a place at the finals.

Index